Writing Skills

AGE 7-9

Exercises devised by Simona Sideri
an experienced author and editor who specialises in children's reference books
Illustrated by Pip Adams

About this book

Writing Skills 7-9 forms part of **Learning Rewards**, a home-learning programme designed to help your child succeed at school with the National Curriculum (and with the 5-14 programme in Scotland). It has been extensively researched with parents and teachers.

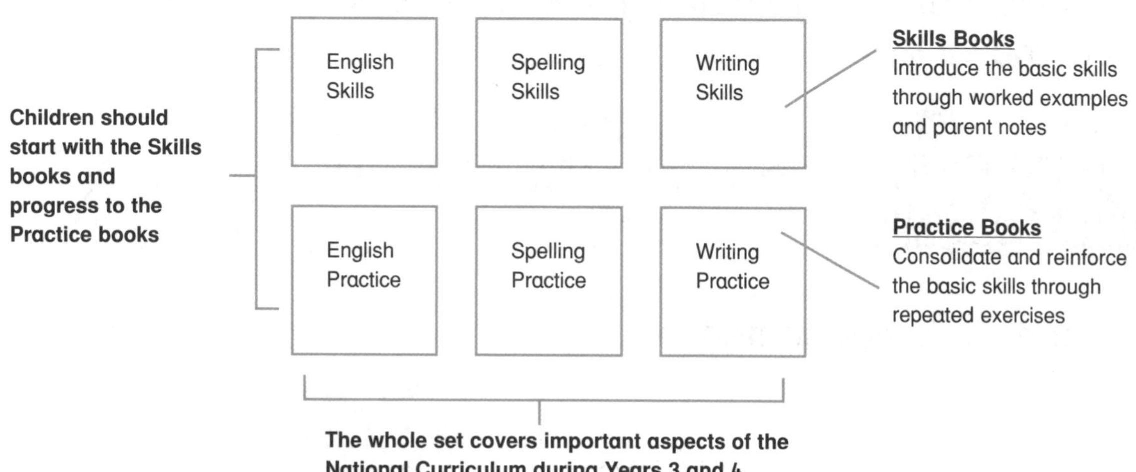

Children should start with the Skills books and progress to the Practice books
English Skills
Spelling Skills
Writing Skills
English Practice
Spelling Practice
Writing Practice
Skills Books
Introduce the basic skills through worked examples and parent notes
Practice Books
Consolidate and reinforce the basic skills through repeated exercises
The whole set covers important aspects of the National Curriculum during Years 3 and 4

How to use this book

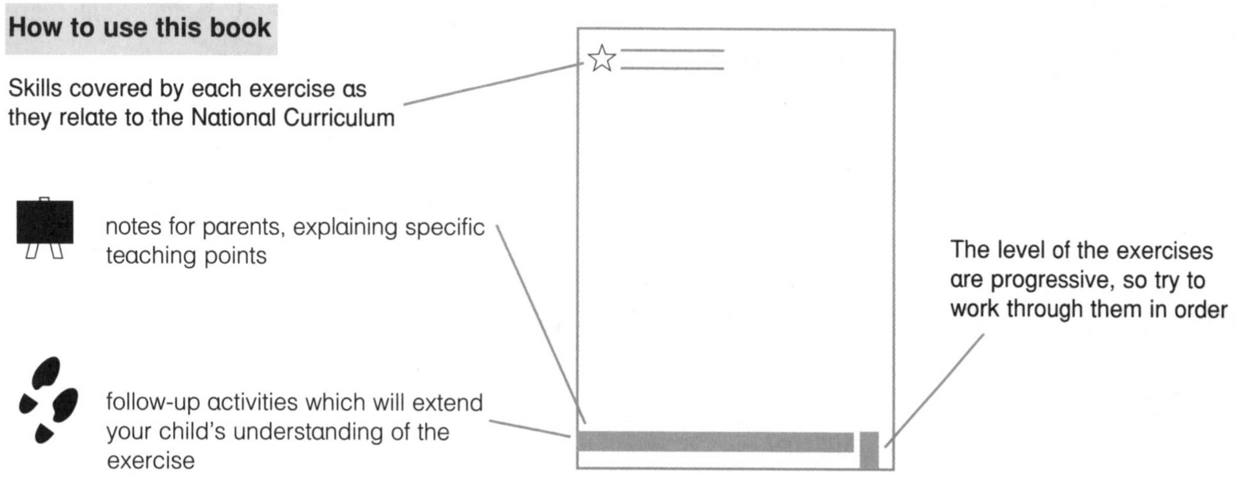

Skills covered by each exercise as they relate to the National Curriculum
notes for parents, explaining specific teaching points
follow-up activities which will extend your child's understanding of the exercise
The level of the exercises are progressive, so try to work through them in order

How you can help

- Work through each page with your child and talk about what is required
- Take note of the information at the bottom of each page and use it to help your child
- Record your child's performance using the progress chart and gold stickers

Copyright © 2002 Egmont Books Ltd.
All rights reserved.

Published in Great Britain in 2002, by Egmont Books Ltd.
239 Kensington High Street, London, W8 6SA.
Printed in Italy
3 5 7 9 10 8 6 4 2

ISBN 0 7498 5567 3

Nouns

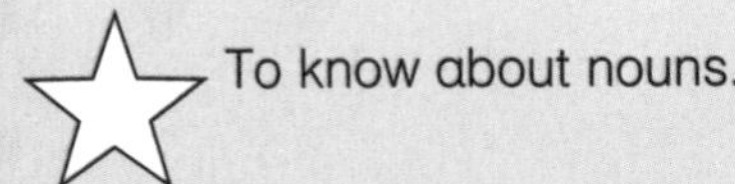

A noun is a thing or a name.

car  town  girl 

If it is the special name of something, we call it a **proper noun** and give it a capital letter:

London  Sally Mount Everest

Circle the nouns in these sentences.

1. The ball crashed through the branches.
2. The old lady ran for the bus waving her stick.
3. I went to London to see my aunt.

Do this puzzle. The answers are all nouns.

Across
1. you sit at it to eat your dinner
4. a step on a ladder
6. you need wind to make it fly
8. animal that lives by rivers

Down
1. large van, or lorry
2. carry things in it
3. eat it or lay it
5. fruit which sounds like two
7. a pet which can guard the house

	1		2		3
4					
				5	
	6				
7					
8					

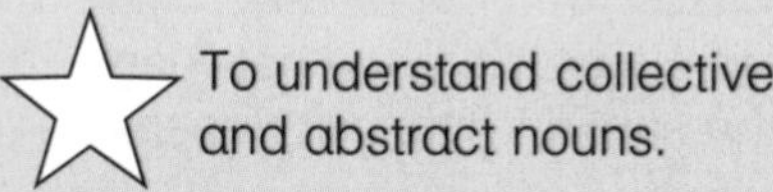
To understand collective and abstract nouns.

Nouns

Collective nouns are names for groups of people, animals or things.

Fill in the gaps with the right collective nouns.

a____________of people
a____________of footballers
a____________of elephants
a____________of bees
a____________of puppies
a____________of flowers
a____________of children
a____________of geese

gang
herd
litter
team
swarm
crowd
bunch
gaggle

Abstract nouns are things which we can't really see or touch.

I look after my health by eating lots of good foods.
Money does not always bring happiness.

Fill each space with the right abstract noun from the list.

After my cat died, I thought my __________ would never go away.

He showed real __________ by rescuing the dog.

An honest person tells the __________.

truth grief courage

Encourage your child to practise different sorts of writing. Look at labels, road signs and adverts and talk about how they are written and why (for example, signs are simple and clear; brand names have to be easy to recognise).

Working with verbs

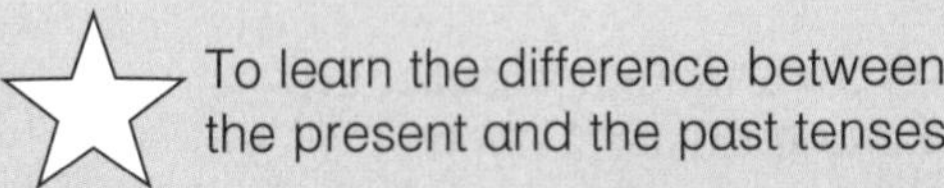

To learn the difference between the present and the past tenses.

Verbs are words which tell us what someone or something is doing or thinking.

Verbs in the present tense tell us about things that are happening now.
The sun is shining.

Verbs in the past tense tell us about things that have already happened.
The sun shone yesterday.

Fill in the past or present of the verbs in brackets. If you are not sure of the spelling, check in a dictionary.

I know a little boy called Jack who ________ (live) on my street. He ________(tell) me this story.

On his way home from school one day he saw some seeds on the ground. They ________ (be) large and ________ (look) unusual. He ________ (take) them home. Then he________(dig) a hole in the ground and ________ (plant) the seeds. Every day he ________ (water) them. After a few weeks bright green shoots ________(push) their way up through the earth. The ________ plant (grow) taller and taller.

Today the plant is so tall it________(reach) the sky. Jack ________(say) he ________ (want) to climb up the trunk and ________ (see) where it ________ (take) him. I don't ________(think) that____ (be) such a good idea.

Write a paragraph of three sentences about what Jack saw at the top of the plant. The first sentence has been written for you.

Yesterday Jack told me he had Climbed the tree.

____

____

____

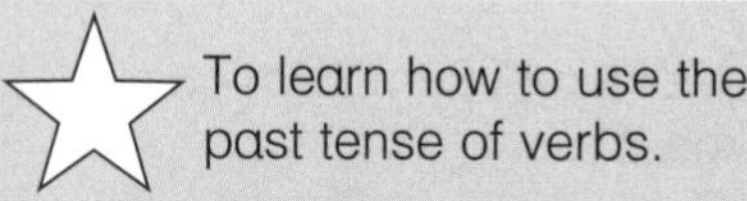
To learn how to use the
past tense of verbs.

The past tense

Most verbs add **-ed** in the past tense:

I open the door. Yesterday, I opened the door.

Fill in the gaps with the past tense of the right verb.

The children__________ some flowers yesterday.
The boys __________ another ice-cream.
I__________ for it everywhere.
The angry girl__________ at her sister.

pick
want
look
shout

Some verbs change completely in the past tense.
You have to learn them:

She sees a plane flying past.
Yesterday, she saw a plane flying past.

Write these sentences in the past tense.

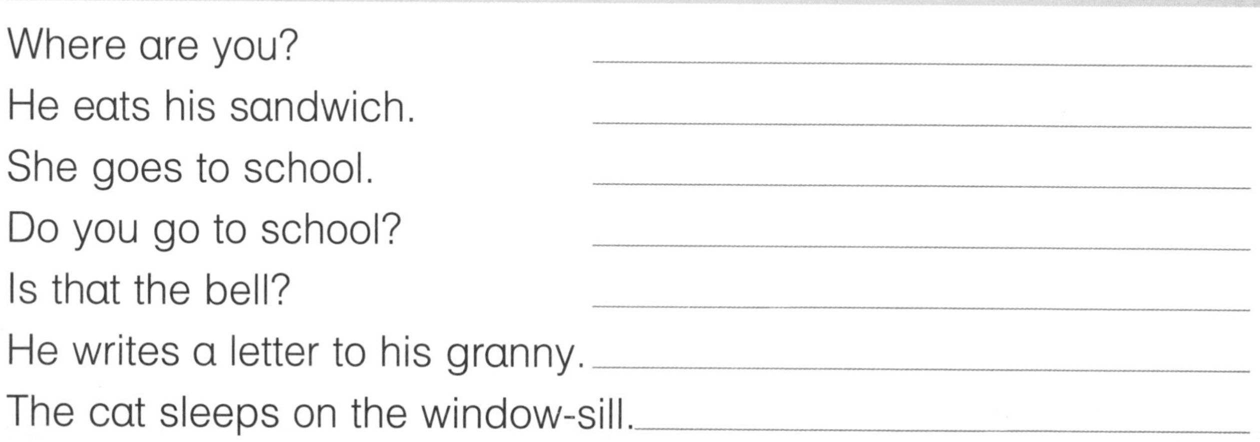

Where are you? __________
He eats his sandwich. __________
She goes to school. __________
Do you go to school? __________
Is that the bell? __________
He writes a letter to his granny. __________
The cat sleeps on the window-sill. __________

Verb formations

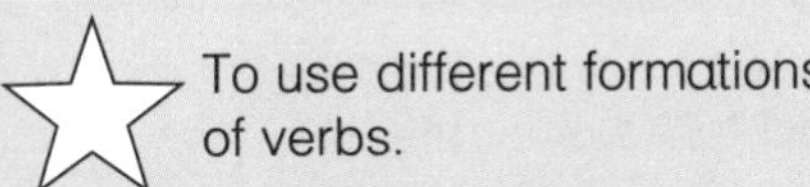

To use different formations of verbs.

Be and **have** are useful verbs. Notice how they change.
Choose your own words to finish these sentences.

I am ______________________.	You have ______________________.
He is ______________________.	She has ______________________.
We are ______________________.	They have ______________________.

These small verbs often go in front of other verbs and change the tense.

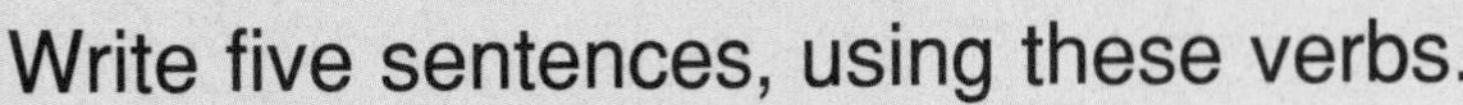

Write five sentences, using these verbs.

I ______________________________.

We ______________________________.

She ______________________________.

It ______________________________.

You ______________________________.

was had finished thinking writing is running were screaming are

Add **s** when you talk about **he**, **she** and **it**.

To learn to use the future tense of verbs.

The future

We use the future tense for things that have not happened yet.

It will rain tomorrow.

Match the two halves of these sentences.

Do you think	to be late.
We will	try not to be noisy.
You will	call you until tomorrow.
I am going	be sorry if it breaks, won't you?
They said they weren't going	to buy myself a book.
I will not	it will rain?

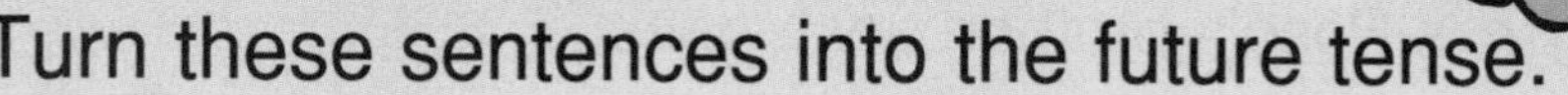

Turn these sentences into the future tense.

It is a wet day, today.

____

I went to the beach.

____

She bought me a present.

____

They lost their seats.

____

Have you seen that film?

____

Pronouns

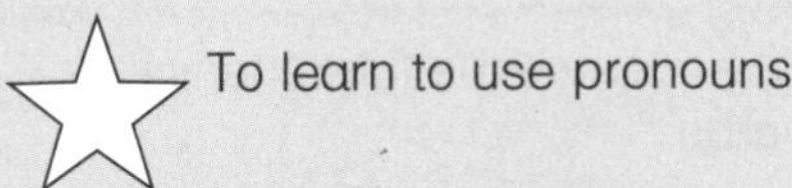
To learn to use pronouns.

You use pronouns so that you don't repeat nouns in your writing.

Dan and Matt went to the match. __________ 're fans.

The girl was sitting on the sofa when __________ heard a noise.

My name's John. __________ live in South Africa.

Ben was sleeping because __________ was tired.

That bottle is empty, but __________ was full this morning.

Rosa and I went to the cinema. __________ loved the film.

Change ten nouns in this story into pronouns.

Rosa goes to school by bus. Rosa doesn't like it, but there's nothing Rosa can do about it. Josh is Rosa's brother. Josh goes to school by bike. Josh is old enough to go by himself. Rosa hopes that when Rosa is old enough Rosa will be able to go by bike too.

The bus is horrible. The bus takes such a long time and Rosa's always late. Every day Rosa waits with her mum at the same bus stop. Every day Rosa and Mum have to wait for ages, but the bus driver is always in a good mood. Even when it is raining the bus driver has a smile for Rosa.

You only use a pronoun when you have just mentioned the noun.

To learn to use possessive pronouns.

Possessive pronouns

My, **your**, **his**, **her**, **its**, **our**, **your** and **their** tell you **who** or **what** a noun belongs to. They are **possessive pronouns**.

Fill in the gaps with the correct possessive pronouns.

Matt's very happy that ________ brother is coming home.
That's ________ bike over there. Do you like it?
________ handle is broken.
Where are ________ parents going?
The children are going to ________ friend's party.
________ bus is late. We'll never get there on time.

There is no apostrophe in **its**!

my your our its his their

You use different possessive pronouns if you don't want to repeat the noun. Fill in the gaps with the correct possessive pronouns.

mine	My bike has five gears and Annie's has six. ________ is faster.
yours	That's not their car. ________ is green.
Hers	I haven't got a red pencil, so that one can't be ________.
ours	Give us back the ball. It's ________ !
Theirs	I haven't got a red pencil, so that one must be ________.

These words don't have an apostrophe!

Your child probably already uses pronouns in his or her speech. Encourage your child to use pronouns in his or her writing.

Adjectives

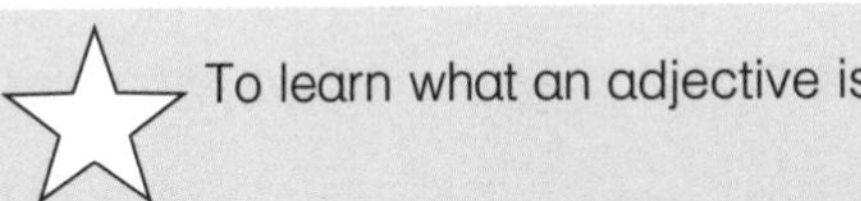
To learn what an adjective is.

An adjective tells us more about a noun.

a small, blue, spotty ball

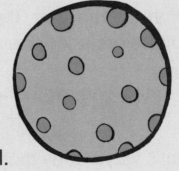

Each adjective tells us something about the ball.

The nouns in this description are underlined. Circle the adjectives.

My house is small but very cosy. It has a grey roof and a new chimney because a huge storm blew the old chimney down. An ancient tree leans towards the house and taps its twisty branches against the red bricks. The narrow garden is full of bright flowers and thick bushes to hide behind.

Can you think of some adjectives to go with these nouns?

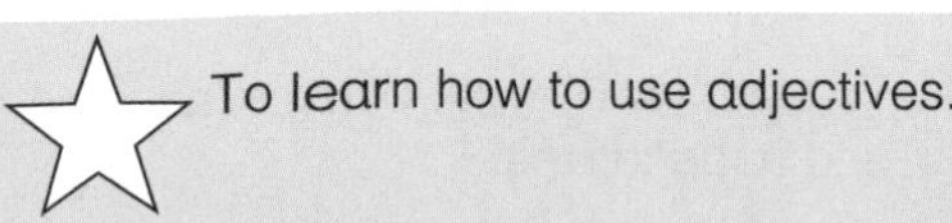
To learn how to use adjectives.

Choosing the best adjectives

If you choose your adjectives very carefully, you can make your reader think or feel whatever you want.

The cat's fur was smooth and silky.
The cat's fur was rough and scratchy.

Read these two passages.
Which passage gives you a clearer picture? Underline the adjectives.

1. The hut was empty. I couldn't see much in it. There was a cupboard in the corner.

2. The hut was cold and dark with a smell of dead spiders. As I peered into the thick blackness, I could just make out the ghostly shape of a wardrobe. With a slow squeak, the door began to open.

Pick your own great adjectives to describe these nouns.

a ______, ______ milkshake   a ______, ______ monster

a ______, ______ storm   a ______, ______ hotdog

a ______, ______ pain in my head   the ______, ______ heat

Big, bigger, biggest

To learn how to use comparatives and superlatives.

The big house.

This house is bigger than that one.

This house is biggest of all.

Who is the oldest?

Which is faster, a cheetah or a donkey?

Which is the softest, a rock, tree or ball?

When you are talking about two things, you must use the **comparative**

I have two coats but I like this one better.
I have three coats and I like this one the best.

Circle the best adjectives in these sentences.

Whose house is **small/smaller/smallest**?
I couldn't be feeling **bad/worse/worst**!
The boy who has won is the **fast/faster/fastest** runner in the school.
That house is **large/larger/largest** than ours.
Don't be so **silly/sillier/silliest**!
I feel **good/well/better** than I did.
He's behaving **bad/worse/worst** than ever.
That joke is **funny/funnier/funniest** than the one you told me yesterday.
That boy can run **fast/faster/fastest** than me.
Do you feel **good/well/better** enough to go to school?

Some important comparisons just have to be learnt.

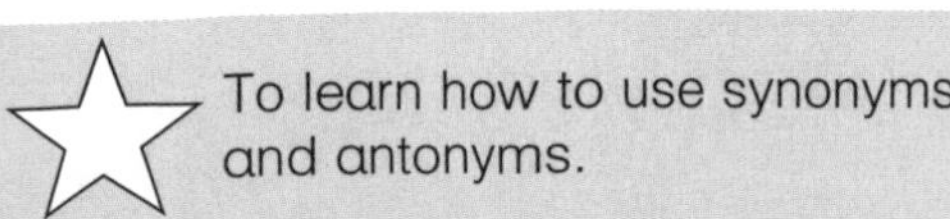

To learn how to use synonyms
and antonyms.

The same or different?

Words that have the same meaning are called **synonyms**.
Fill in the gaps with the verb which means the same as the others.

stroll	amble	wander	________
jog	gallop	dash	________
say	talk	remark	________
scream	roar	cry	________
look	notice	glance	________

run shout
walk see
speak

Write each sentence, replacing the adjective with another one.
Your adjective must mean the same as the one you are replacing.

There is an **enormous** tree in their garden.

____

She said their room was very **messy**.

____

The **evil** magician cast his spell.

____

That was a **delicious** meal!

____

Words that have the opposite meaning are called **antonyms**.
Write the opposite of these words.

go	________	new	________	quickly	________
weak	________	dirty	________	big	________
happy	________	short	________	false	________
bad	________	young	________	frown	________
slow	________	warm	________	quiet	________

Adverbs

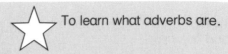

☆ To learn what adverbs are.

Adverbs are words that tell us about verbs or adjectives. The verbs are in boxes and the adverbs are underlined:

The dog

[barked] loudly.

loudly tells us **how** the dog barked

The boy

[ran] quickly.

quickly tells us **how** the boy ran

The verbs are in boxes again. Can you underline the adverbs?

1. I [lay] comfortably on the beach, [listening] happily to the sounds of the waves [lapping] gently.

2. The customers [waited] impatiently for the shopkeeper slowly [to unlock] the shop. 'Hurry up!' one of them [shouted] rudely.

3. Her eyes suddenly [opened] enormously wide.
   She [looked] hopefully at the huge ice-cream.

Your child will learn about these parts of speech at school. Help him or her become familiar with grammatical terms.

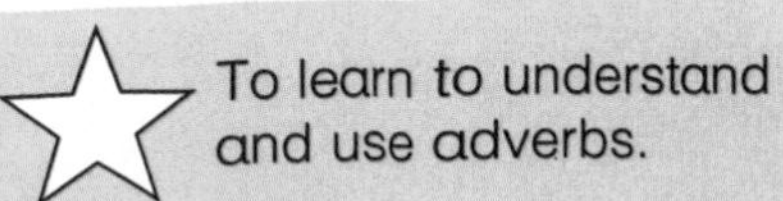
To learn to understand and use adverbs.

Using adverbs

Match each verb on the left to a suitable adverb on the right.

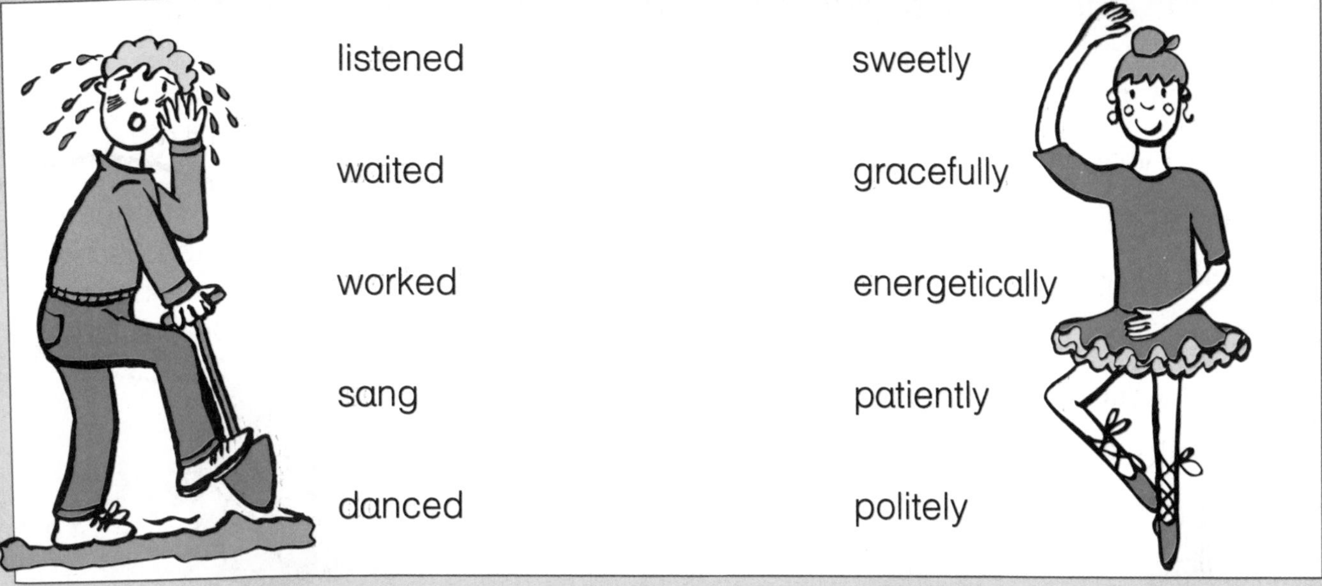

listened	sweetly
waited	gracefully
worked	energetically
sang	patiently
danced	politely

Fill the spaces with the adverbs below. Use each one only once.

The waves crashed ______________ on the sand. A small boat tossed ______________ in the distance, as the grey sea battered it ______________ .

dangerously	noisily	cruelly

The adjectives and adverbs make the picture so clear that you can draw it.

Conjunctions

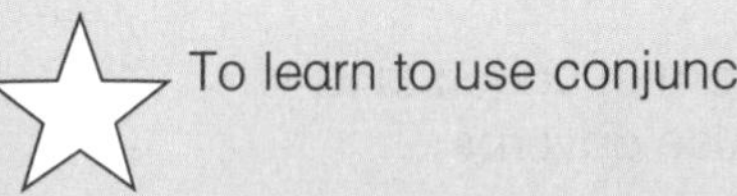
To learn to use conjunctions.

Conjunctions are words that join two ideas.
Fill in the gaps in these sentences, using the right conjunctions from the box.

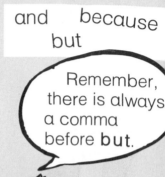

and because but

The girl was yawning, ________ she wasn't tired.
I want some trifle, ________ without cream, please.
I'm skipping ________ I'm in a good mood.
In class, the boys ________ girls worked hard.
The boy didn't speak ________ he was shy.
The children's mother ________ their grandfather came to the show.

Remember, there is always a comma before **but**.

Write each sentence, using the best conjunction.

I lied **so/because/when** I am feeling a bit guilty.

____

They had their supper **while/when/if** watching TV.

____

Will you tell me **when/if/before** I promise?

____

I went for a walk **while/before/when** breakfast.

____

Do you want to go to football **when/after/then** school?

____

First I looked right and **when/then/if** I looked left.

____

She jumped **when/if/so** the lightning flashed.

____

Sentences

To learn to write clear sentences.

A sentence begins with a capital letter and ends with a full stop. It contains a verb, and someone or something to be the subject of the verb.

The exhausted man trudged slowly up the hill.
(subject) (verb)

Write some sentences about your home and family or school and friends.

1. ______________________________
2. ______________________________
3. ______________________________

A sentence must not just go on and on. Break this sentence up into four shorter sentences, using full-stops.

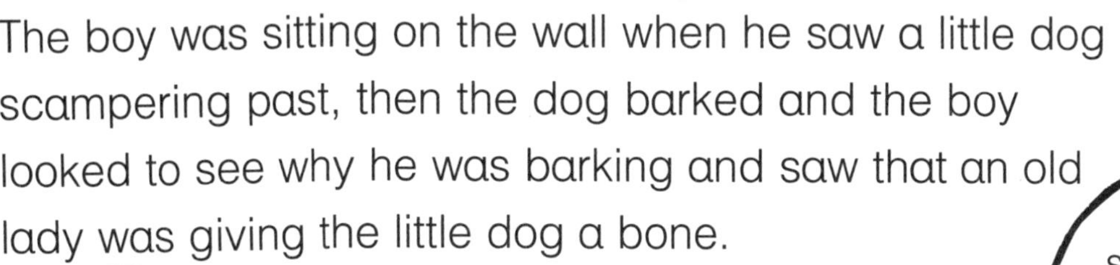

The boy was sitting on the wall when he saw a little dog scampering past, then the dog barked and the boy looked to see why he was barking and saw that an old lady was giving the little dog a bone.

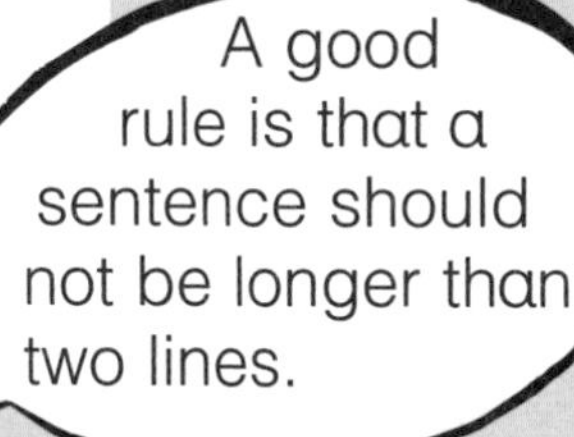

A good rule is that a sentence should not be longer than two lines.

Paragraphs

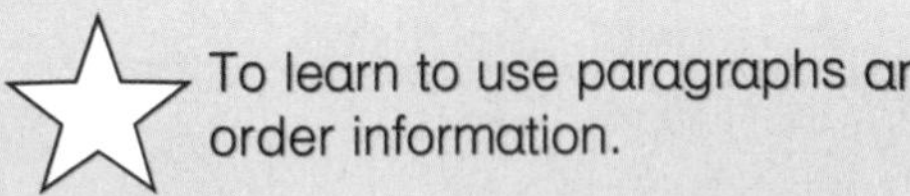

To learn to use paragraphs and order information.

We break up our writing into paragraphs. Each new idea or subject starts a new paragraph. A new paragraph always starts on a new line.

~~My~~ name is Sarah and I am nine years old. I have brown ~~hare~~ hair and brown eyes. ~~I am good at sports~~ I am tall for my age.

I live with my mother ~~who is really nice~~ and my ~~horrible~~ younger brother Simon who is always annoying me and

Oour house is not very big but close to the river and we live in M~~a~~anchester.

My name is Sarah and I am nine years old. I have brown hair and brown eyes. I am tall for my age.

I live with my mother and my younger brother Simon. Our house is not very big, but it is close to the river. We live in Manchester.

The first paragraph talks about Sarah; the second is about Sarah's family.

Write two or three paragraphs about things that make you happy and sad. Take some time to think about what you want to write.

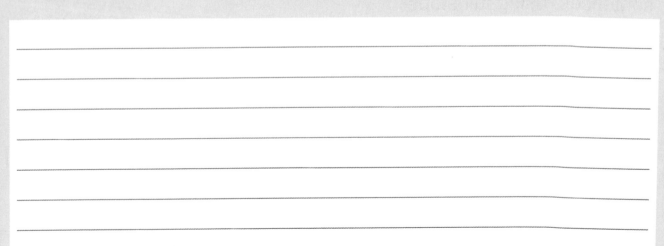

Share with your child any difficulties you have with writing. It helps to let him or her know that even adults have to think about what they write.

Look at your child's writing and encourage him or her to think of other things to say and better words to use.

To learn how to form questions.

Questions

A question is a sentence that needs an answer.
Questions end with a question mark.

That girl is her sister.	Is that girl her sister?
The shops are near the school.	Are the shops near the school?

Turn these sentences into questions.

That car is very fast. ______

Lemons are fruit. ______

She is good at sports. ______

Elephants are very large. ______

Remember to start every question with a capital letter.

Some questions start with **Do** or **Does**.

You know him.	Do you know him?
He likes pasta.	Does he like pasta?

Turn these sentences into questions.

You like eating chips. ______

Their dog runs fast. ______

He reads a lot. ______

My desk looks tidy. ______

I do, you do, we do, they do, he does, she does, it does.

Commas

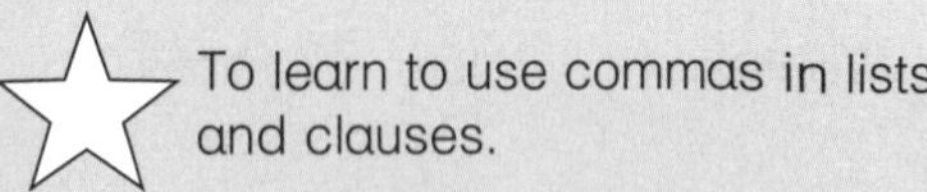
To learn to use commas in lists and clauses.

We put commas between lists of adjectives.

There should be no comma before **and**.

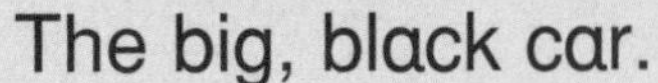
The big, black car.

A funny, hairy, blue and white monster.

We use commas to separate other things in lists, too.
He walked the dog, cleaned the car, went to the shops and made tea.

And we also use commas if a sentence has more than one idea in it.
He loved dogs, even though he had never had one of his own.

Put commas in all the right places in these sentences.

The tall thin smartly-dressed man wears glasses.

I love reading swimming cycling and gardening.

Gemma ran down the road looking from left to right all the time.

The horse escaped from its field which was the farmer's fault.

I grow roses my mother grows vegetables and my brother grows peas.

Help your child to look out for commas in his or her reading. Encourage him or her to listen for the short pause that marks a comma, and how it differs from the longer pause of a full stop. If your child notices commas when reading he or she will learn to use them in his or her writing.

To learn to use apostrophes.

Apostrophes

Apostrophes tell you that something belongs to someone.

the girl's cat

the boy's bicycle

the ________ bag
the ________ trunk
the ________ basket
the ________ tooth

Sometimes we join two words together and miss out a letter.
We put an apostrophe in the place of the missing letter.
Fill in the missing words in these sentences.

His mother just rang to say ________ sick.
________ very happy to see you again.
________ all leaving the classroom.
What do you think ________ doing?
________ a beautiful day.

I'm he's It's you're We're

Add the ten missing apostrophes.

Oscar is seven years old. He has a dog. The dogs fur is brown. His names Buster. Hes a good dog. Busters tongue hangs out when he pants. Its pink and wet. Chloe is Oscars older sister. Shes ten. Theyre at the same school. Chloes hair is long. Busters her dog too.

Help your child to spot apostrophes and listen out for the tell-tale 's' sign at the end of nouns (John's, Mary's...).

Apostrophes

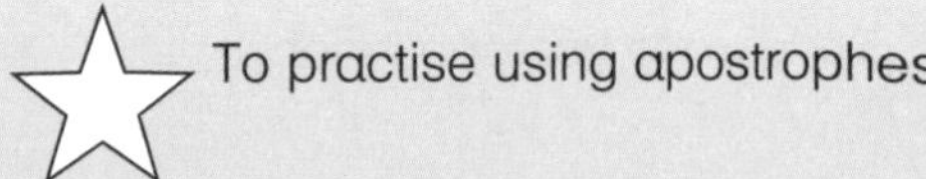
To practise using apostrophes.

Use the pictures to help you fill in the missing words.
The first one has been done for you.

Remember the apostrophe and **s**.

the boy's book
the girl ______
Mum ______
the teacher ______

If the owner is plural, put the apostrophe after the plural word.

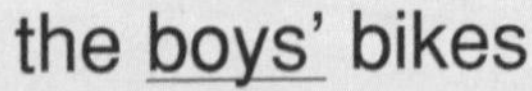

the boys' bikes

the girls' bikes

Use the pictures to help you add the apostrophes.
Be careful with the 3rd one!

the horses hooves
the lambs wool
the childrens shoes
the cats whiskers
the girls box

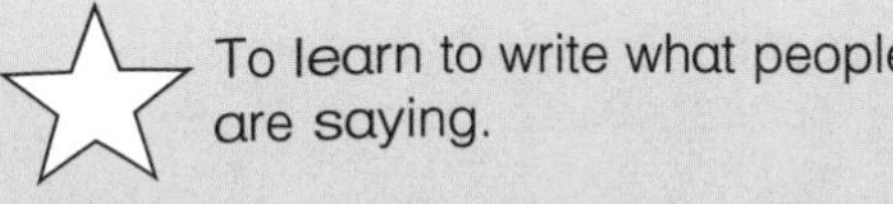

To learn to write what people are saying.

Speech marks

To show that people are speaking, you put speech marks “ ” around their words.

The boy said, “I’m hungry.”
“I’m hungry,” said the boy.

Notice how the full stop appears at the very end of the sentence.

Put speech marks around Amy’s words.

Well, that’s too bad, answered Amy. It’s ages until lunch.

This story has been written without any speech marks.
Add them in the correct places.

Remember, each person’s speech starts on a new line.

Everyone was at the playground except Emma and Varinda.
It’s not fair, said Emma.
No, it’s not, said Varinda. It’s not fair at all.
The girls felt sad. Emma looked at Varinda. Varinda looked at Emma.
Actually, I think it’s fair, said Emma.
I know, agreed Varinda. We shouldn’t have been mean to Jessica.
Let’s make her a card to say we’re sorry, said Emma. And that is what they did.

Help your child make up some scripts, based on a family mealtime or someone’s visit. Help him or her write down what was said and then put it together with all the correct punctuation.

Narration

☆ To write about daily events in sequence.

In the morning...

I get up in the morning and have a wash.

Then I put on my pants and my T-shirt.

Next I put on socks and trousers.

Sometimes I wear a jumper too.

Then I go downstairs and eat cereal with milk.

Afterwards I brush my teeth.

I put on my shoes and my coat. I'm ready for school.

Write down what you do in the morning.

First I ______________________________

______________________________.

Next I ______________________________

______________________________.

Then I ______________________________

______________________________.

Encourage your child to tell stories in sequence. After reading a story to your child, ask him/her to tell you what happened, in order.

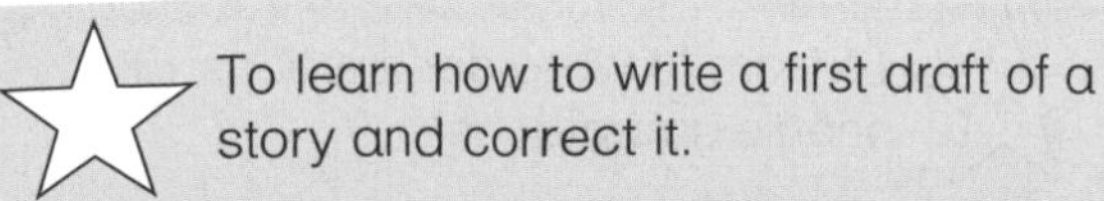

To learn how to write a first draft of a story and correct it.

Story time

When you write something, it's important to do a rough draft first. Then you can read it and make any changes or corrections. You might think of better ways to explain what you want to say, and you will probably also find some mistakes.

Here is a first draft of the beginning of a story. First, correct all the mistakes you can find.

The childern lookd at each other with fear in there eyes. The old deserted house creaked in the wind as darkness fell on its broken roof. Their thinn clothes would'nt protect them from the cold night.

Joe heard rustling sound he didn't no what it was. He thought it mite be a rat, He shivered. Jess was only 6 and he didn't want her to know he was frightened. He was two years older and he was in charge. He had left his coat at home and he wished that he hadn't. He was cold. He shivered in his torn t-shirt.

The teo blond-haired children huddled together. Suddenly, Jess whispered, 'Come on Joe. We can't stay her all night. We have to find our way back.'

Can you find other bits you would like to change? There are some problems with the second paragraph. Have I repeated myself? Is there something which should be in a different paragraph?

Redraft the second paragraph, making it better in any way you like.

Tell a good story

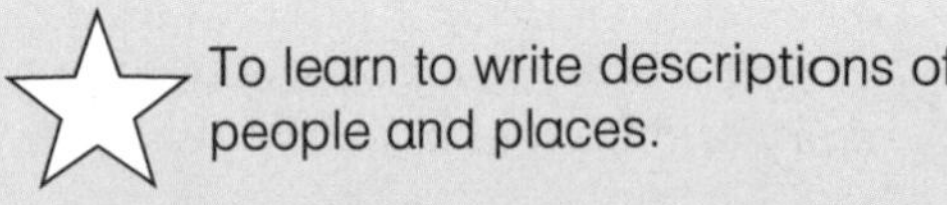

To learn to write descriptions of people and places.

A good storyteller describes the scene – the place where the story happens – and tells the reader who the characters are, what they look like and where they live.

Good descriptions make a story come to life and help keep the reader interested.

Look again at the story on page 25. Describe Joe and Jess. What do they look like? What colour is their hair? How old are they? What are they wearing?

Describe the house. What information does the writer give you about the house? Can you think of something else which you imagine the house is like?

Encourage your child to talk about places he or she knows: Where are they? What sort of buildings are there? Talk about people he or she knows: What colour are their eyes ... their hair? What are they wearing? The more your child describes, the more ideas he or she will have when writing.

To develop characters in a story.

Writing a story

The people in a story are called the characters.
Who are they? What do they look like? What are they wearing?

He was a fat dragon with scales that dripped with green slime.
His eyes were small, but shiny. Hot jets of fire spouted out of his nose.
He was very, very angry.

Write five sentences about a made-up person. Use the pictures for ideas. You may like to give your character the girl's nose or the man's hair-style. Use adjectives to describe your character and make them sound interesting.

What is your character like as a person? Mean or generous? Happy or sad? Confident or worried about things? Jot down some characteristics, and decide what is the most important thing about your character.

Rhymes and other word sounds

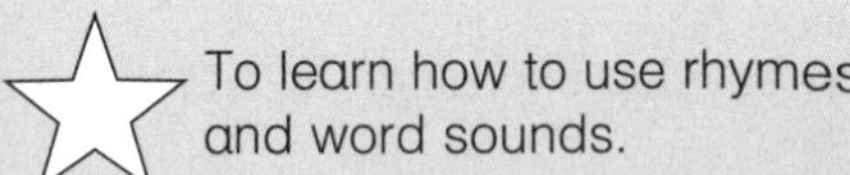

To learn how to use rhymes
and word sounds.

Poetry uses language in special ways. Poems often rhyme.

I am so happy that
I have put on a hat.

Match the words that rhyme.

annoy shoulder respect connect
youth truth destroy boulder

Write two rhyming sentences.

The rhyme is on the last word.

Poets also use **alliteration**. Alliteration is when words that start with the same sound follow one after another.

The shellfish shines and shimmers and is sure to follow Sheila.

Think of two or more words that alliterate with each of these words.

dragon
snake
bear

Alliteration works with the first sound of the word, not just the first letter.

Onomatopoeia (say it o-no-ma-toe-pee-a) is when a word sounds like the thing it describes.

sizzle crash bang

Write some more onomatopoeic words. Try to make up some of your own.

Help your child think of onomatopoeic words and make up his or her own. When you see any, point them out.

To learn to write a simple letter.

Writing letters

25 Lansdowne Road
Plymouth
22nd February

Dear Adriana,

How are you? I'm very well. I didn't write earlier because I was very busy.

It's great here. I like my new school and have made lots of friends. A boy called Jerry lives next door. He's very good at sports and maths too. He likes animals just as we do, but even more. He says he's going to be a vet when he grows up.

I am still thinking about being a writer. Do you want me to send you the story I am writing when I finish it?

Write back soon and tell me about what you are doing.

lots of love
Shane xx

Pretend you are Adriana and write back to Shane. Adriana's address is on the envelope Shane sent her.

2, Harmer's Lane
Little Lenwade
Suffolk
27th February

Write letters with your child to friends and family who live far away. Remind your child to include his or her own address and the date. Help your child to plan the letters and correct the first drafts.

Written instructions

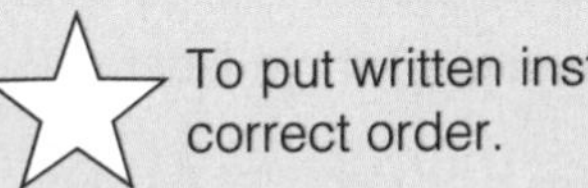

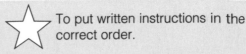

To put written instructions in the correct order.

You need:

2 slices of bread
butter
I lettuce leaf
2 slices of cheese
some pickle

These instructions are in the wrong order. Number them in the right order.

	Enjoy your sandwich!
	Spread pickle on the cheese.
	Lay the lettuce on top of one slice of bread.
	Put the cheese on top of the lettuce.
	Place the other slice of bread on the top.
	Use a knife to butter both slices of bread.
	Make sure you have all the ingredients listed above.

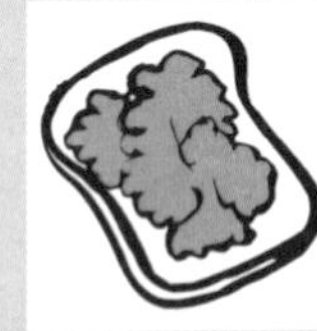

Write down three fillings which you like in your sandwiches.

I. ______________________________

2. ______________________________

3. ______________________________

Help your child think about the order in which things are done. Talk about why we do things in a certain order. Think about meals (dessert follows the main course; the steps involved in making a cup of tea), and other everyday activities (routines at home and at school).

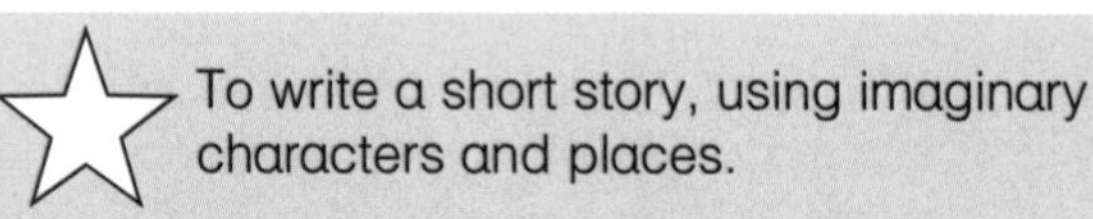

To write a short story, using imaginary characters and places.

Writing for pleasure

Now you can write a great story or poem, using what you have learnt. This page is to help you sort your ideas and plan what to write.

Who is your main character or characters?

____

Set your story or poem on a deserted beach. First jot down some ideas about what the beach looks and feels like. What's the weather like? What can you see? Why is your character there?

____

____

____

____

Now write down some interesting adjectives, verbs and adverbs which you would like to use.

____

____

____

____

Get a fresh piece of paper and start your first draft. When you are happy with it, copy it onto smart paper and stick it on your wall. You are a writer!

Answers

page 2
ball, branches, lady, bus, stick, I, London, aunt
Across: 1. table, 4. rung, 6. kite, 8. otter
Down: 1. truck, 2. bag, 3. egg, 5. pear, 7. dog

page 3
crowd, team, herd, swarm, litter, bunch, gang, gaggle
grief, courage, truth

page 4
lives, told, were, looked, took, dug, planted, watered, pushed, grew,
reaches, says, wants, see, takes,
think, is

page 5
picked, wanted, looked, shouted
Where were you?; He ate his sandwich.
She went to school.; Did you go to school?;
Was that the bell?; He wrote a letter to his granny.; The cat slept on the window-sill.

page 7
Do you think it will rain?; We will try not to be noisy.; You will be sorry if it breaks, won't you?; I am going to buy myself a book.; They said they weren't going to be late.; I will not call you until tomorrow.
It is going to/will be a wet day tomorrow.
I am going to/will go to the beach.
She is going to/will buy me a present.
They are going to/will lose their seats.
Are you going to/Will you see that film?

page 8
They, she, I, he, it, We
Rosa goes to school by bus. She doesn't like it, but there's nothing she can do about it. Josh is Rosa's brother. He goes to school by bike. He is old enough to go by himself. Rosa hopes that when she is old enough she will be able to go by bike too.
The bus is horrible. It takes such a long time and Rosa's always late. Every day she waits with her mum at the same bus stop. Every day they have to wait for ages, but the bus driver is always in a good mood. Even when it is raining he has a smile for Rosa.

page 9
his, my, Its, your, their, Our
Hers, Theirs, mine, ours, yours

page 10
small, cosy, grey, new, huge, old, ancient, twisty, red, narrow, bright, thick

page 11
empty, cold, dark, dead, thick, ghostly, slow
The second passage gives a clearer picture because it has lots of adjectives
that tell us about the nouns: cold, dark, dead, thick, ghostly, slow.

page 12
Gran, a cheetah, a ball
smallest, worse, fastest, larger, silly,
better, worse, funnier, faster, well

page 13
walk, run, speak, shout, see
huge/big/large, untidy, wicked/bad, tasty
stop, old, slowly, strong, clean, small, sad, long/tall, true, good, old, smile, fast, cold, noisy

page 14
1. comfortably, happily, gently
2. impatiently, slowly, rudely
3. suddenly, enormously, hopefully

page 15
listened politely, waited patiently,
worked energetically, sang sweetly,
danced gracefully
noisily, dangerously, cruelly

page 16
but, but, because, and, because, and
so, while, if, before, after, then, when

page 17
The boy was sitting on the wall when he saw a little dog scampering past. Then the dog barked. The boy looked to see why he was barking. He saw that an old lady was giving the little dog a bone.

page 19
Is that car very fast?
Are lemons fruit?
Is she good at sports?
Are elephants very large?
Do you like eating chips?
Does their dog run fast?
Does he read a lot?
Does my desk look tidy?

page 20
The tall, thin, smartly-dressed man wears glasses.
I love reading, swimming, cycling and gardening.
Gemma ran down the road, looking from left to right all the time.
The horse escaped from its field, which was the farmer's fault.
I grow roses, my mother grows vegetables and my brother grows peas.

page 21
girl's, elephant's, dog's, boy's
he's, I'm, We're, you're, It's
Oscar is seven years old. He is a dog. The dog's fur is brown. His name's Buster. He's a good dog. Buster's tongue hangs out when he pants. It's pink and wet. Chloe is Oscar's older sister. She's ten. They're at the same school. Chloe's hair is long. Buster's her dog too.

page 22
the boy's book, the girl's dog, Mum's car, the teacher's briefcase
the horses' hooves, the lambs' wool, the children's shoes, the cats' whiskers, the girls' box

page 23
"Well, that's too bad," answered Amy.
"It's ages until lunch."
Everyone was at the playground except Emma and Varinda.
"It's not fair," said Emma.
"No it's not," said Varinda. "It's not fair at all."
The girls felt sad. Emma looked at Varinda.
Varinda looked at Emma.
"Actually, I think it's fair," said Emma.
"I know," agreed Varinda. "We shouldn't have been mean to Jessica."
"Let's make her a card to say we're sorry," said Emma. And that is what they did.

page 25
The children looked at each other with fear in their eyes. The old deserted house creaked in the wind as darkness fell on its broken roof. Their thin clothes wouldn't protect them from the cold night.
Joe heard a rustling sound. He didn't know what it was. He thought it might be a rat. He shivered. Jess was only 6 and he didn't want her to know he was frightened. He was two years older and he was in charge. He had left his coat at home and he wished that he hadn't. He was cold. He shivered in his torn T-shirt.
The two blond-haired children huddled together. Suddenly, Jess whispered, 'Come on Joe. We can't stay here all night. We have to find our way back.'

page 28
annoy-destroy, youth-truth, shoulder-boulder, respect-connect

page 30
1. Make sure you have all the ingredients listed above.
2. Use a knife to butter both slices of bread.
3. Lay the lettuce on top of one slice of bread.
4. Put the cheese on top of the lettuce.
5. Spread pickle on the cheese.
6. Place the other slice of bread on top.
7. Enjoy your sandwich!